CorelDraw
Keyboard Shortcuts

By

U. C-Abel Books.

Published by U. C-Abel Books

All Rights Reserved

First Edition: 2017

ISBN-13: 978-1544038476
ISBN-10: 154403847X

Published by U. C-Abel Books.

Table of Contents

Acknowledgement.

We return all glory to God Almighty for enabling us to bring this work to this point.

We sincerely appreciate the great company called Corel Corporation for their hard work and way of reasoning in terms of providing their customers with helpful programs and resources, and for helping us with some of the tips and keyboard shortcuts included in this book. We also remember our lovely readers who are never tired of reading our publications.

We really wish you well.

Dedication

We pleasurably dedicate this title to users of CorelDraw all over the world.

Introduction

After thinking of how to help computer users become more productive in their operation of computers and various fields, it came to our knowledge that there is a smart option many computer users ignore easily and that part has a high yielding capacity that is known to just few people.

We went into a deep research to broaden our knowledge of key combination and found it very helpful, then we started this series "Shortcut Matters" including tips, techniques, keyboard shortcuts, and packaging the title in a way it will attract readers and get a high rating class.

As people who love keyboard shortcuts we treat each topic plainly in an easy-to-read way even to the understanding of a lay man.

Relax and make your mind ready for learning as we go.

What to Know Before You Begin.

General Notes.

1. Most of the keyboard shortcuts you will see in this book refer to the U.S. keyboard layout. Keys for other layouts might not correspond exactly to the keys on a U.S. keyboard. Keyboard shortcuts for laptop computers might also differ.

2. It is important to note that when using shortcuts to perform any command, you should make sure the target area is active, if not, you may get a wrong result. Example, if you want to highlight all texts you must make sure the text field is active and if an object, make sure the object area is active. The active area is always known by the location where the cursor of your computer blinks.

3. On a Mac keyboard, the Command key is denoted with the ⌘ symbol.

4. If a function key doesn't work on your Mac as you expect it to, press the Fn key in addition to the function key. If you don't want to press the Fn key every time, you can change your Apple system preferences.

5. The plus (+) sign that comes in the middle of keyboard shortcuts simply means the keys are meant to be combined or held down together not to be added as one of the shortcut keys. In a case where plus sign is needed; it will be duplicated (++).

6. Many keyboards assign special functions to function keys, by default. To use the function key for other purposes, you have to press Fn+the function key.
7. For keyboard shortcuts in which you press one key immediately followed by another key, the keys are separated by a comma (,).

8. For chapters that have more than one topic, search for "A fresh topic" to see the beginning of a topic, and "End of Topic" to see the end of a topic.

9. It is also important to note that the keyboard shortcuts listed in this book are to be used in CorelDraw.

10. To get more information on this title visit ucabelbooks.wordpress.com and search the site using keywords related to it.

11. Our chief website is under construction.

Some Short Forms You Will Find in This Book and Their Full Meaning.

Here are short forms used in this CorelDraw Keyboard Shortcuts book and their full meaning.

1.	Win	-	Windows logo key
2.	Tab	-	Tabulate Key
3.	Shft	-	Shift Key
4.	Prt sc	-	Print Screen
5.	Num Lock	-	Number Lock Key
6.	F	-	Function Key
7.	Esc	-	Escape Key
8.	Ctrl	-	Control Key
9.	Caps Lock	-	Caps Lock Key
10.	Alt	-	Alternate Key

CHAPTER 1.

Fundamental Knowledge of Keyboard Shortcuts.

Without the existence of the keyboard, there wouldn't have been anything like keyboard shortcuts so in this chapter we will learn a little about the computer keyboard before moving to keyboard shortcuts.

1. Definition of Computer Keyboard.

This is an input device that is used to send data to computer memory.

Sketch of a Keyboard

1.1 Types of Keyboard.

   i. Standard (Basic) Keyboard.

  ii. Enhanced (Extended) Keyboard.

   i. **Standard Keyboard:** This is a keyboard designed during the 1800s for mechanical typewriters with just 10 function keys (F keys) placed at the left side of it.

  ii. **Enhanced Keyboard:** This is the current 101 to 102-key keyboard that is included in almost all the personal computers (PCs) of nowadays, which has 12 function keys, usually at the top side of it.

Function Keys

Numeric Keys

Alphabetic keys

1.2 Segments of the keyboard

- Numeric keys.
- Alphabetic keys.
- Punctuation keys.
- Windows Logo key.
- Function keys.
- Special keys.

Numeric Keys: Numeric keys are keys with numbers from **0 - 9**.

Alphabetic Keys: These are keys that have alphabets on them, ranging from **A** to **Z**.

Punctuation Keys: These are keys of the keyboard used for punctuation, examples include comma, full stop, colon, question marks, hyphen, etc.

Windows Logo Key: A key on Microsoft Computer keyboard with its logo displayed on it. Search for this ⊞ on your keyboard.

Apple Key: This also known as Command key is a modifier key that you can find on an Apple keyboard. It usually has the image of an apple or command logo on it. Search for this on your Apple keyboard ⌘

Function Keys: These are keys that have **F** on them which are usually combined with other keys. They are F1 - F12, and are also in the class called *Special Keys*.

Special Keys: These are keys that perform special functions. They include: Tab, Ctrl, Caps lock, Insert, Prt sc, alt gr, Shift, Home, Num lock, Esc, and many others. Special keys differ according to the type of computer involved. In some keyboard layout, especially laptops, the keys that turn the speaker on/off, the one that increases/decreases volume, the key that turns the computer Wifi on/off are also special keys.

Other Special Keys Worthy of Note.

Enter Key: This is located at the right-hand corner of most keyboards. It is used to send messages to the computer to execute commands, in most cases it is used to mean "Ok" or "Go".

Escape Key (ESC): This is the first key on the upper left of most keyboards. It is used to cancel routines, close menus and select options such as **Save** according to circumstances.

Control Key (CTRL): It is located on the bottom row of the left and right hand side of the keyboard. They also work with the function keys to execute commands using Keyboard shortcuts (key combinations).

Alternate Key (ALT): It is located on the bottom row also of some keyboard, very close to the CTRL key on both side of the keyboard. It enables many editing functions to be accomplished by using some keystroke combinations on the keyboard.

Shift Key: This adds to the roles of function keys. In addition, it enables the use of alternative function of a particular button (key), especially, those with more than one function on a key. E.g. use of capital letters, symbols, and numbers.

1.3. Selecting/Highlighting With Keyboard.

This is a highlighting method or style where data is selected using the computer keyboard instead of a computer mouse.

To do this:

- Move your cursor to the text or object you want to highlight, make sure that area is active,
- Hold down the shift key with one finger,
- Then use another finger to move the arrow key that points to the direction you want to highlight.

1.4 The Operating Modes Of The Keyboard.

Just like the computer mouse, keyboard has two operating modes. The two modes are Text Entering Mode and Command Mode.

a. **Text Entering Mode:** this mode gives the operator/user the opportunity to type text.
b. **Command Mode:** this is used to command the operating system/software/application to execute commands in certain ways.

2. Ways To Improve In Your Typing Skill.

1. Put Your Eyes Off The Keyboard.

This is the aspect of keyboard usage that many don't find funny because they always ask. "How can I put my eyes off the keyboard when I am running away from the occurrence of errors on my file?" My aim is to be fast, is this not going to slow me down?

Of course, there will be errors and at the same time your speed will slow down but the motive behind the introduction to this method is to make you faster than you are. Looking at your keyboard while you type can make you get a sore neck, it is better you learn to touch type because the more you type with your eyes fixed on the screen instead of the keyboard, the faster you become.

An alternative to keeping your eyes off your keyboard is to use the *"Das Keyboard Ultimate"*.

2. Errors Challenge You

It is better to fail than to not try at all. Not trying at all is an attribute of the weak and lazybones. When you make mistakes, try again because errors are opportunities for improvement.

3. Good Posture (Position Yourself Well).

Do not adopt an awkward position while typing. You should get everything on your desk organized or arranged before sitting to type. Your posture while typing contributes to your speed and productivity.

4. Practice

Here is the conclusion of everything said above. You have to practice your shortcuts constantly. The practice alone is a way of improvement. "Practice brings improvement". Practice always.

2.1 Software That Will Help You Improve Your Typing Skill.

There are several Software programs for typing that both kids and adults can use for their typing skill. Here is a list of software that can help you improve in your typing: Mavis Beacon, Typing Instructor, Mucky Typing Adventure, Rapid Tying Tutor, Letter Chase Tying Tutor, Alice Touch Typing Tutor and many more. Personally, I love Mavis Beacon.

To learn typing using MAVIS BEACON, install Mavis Beacon software to your computer, start with keyboard lesson, then move to games. Games like ***Penguin Crossing, Creature Lab***, or ***Space Junk*** will help you become a professional in typing. Typing and keyboard shortcuts work hand-in-hand.

Sketch of a computer mouse

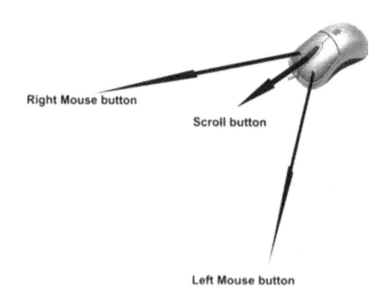

Right Mouse button

Scroll button

Left Mouse button

3. Mouse:

This is an oval-shaped portable input device with three buttons for scrolling, left clicking, and right clicking that enables work to be done effectively on a computer. The plural form of mouse is mice.

3.1 Types of Computer Mouse

- Mechanical Mouse.
- Optical Mechanical Mouse (Optomechanical).
- Laser Mouse.
- Optical Mouse.

- BlueTrack Mouse.

3.2 Forms of Clicking:

Left Clicking: This is the process of clicking the left side button of the mouse. It can also be called *clicking* without the addition of *left*.

Right Clicking: It is the process of clicking the right side button of a computer mouse.

Double Clicking: It is the process of clicking the left side button two times (twice) and immediately.

Triple Clicking: It is the process of clicking the left side button three times (thrice) and immediately.

Double clicking is used to select a word while triple clicking is used to select a sentence or paragraph.

Scroll Button: It is the little key attached to the mouse that looks like a tiny wheel. It takes you up and down a page when moved.

3.3 Mouse Pad: This is a small soft mat that is placed under the mouse to make it have a free movement.

3.4 Laptop Mouse Touchpad

This unlike the mouse we explained above is not external, rather it is inbuilt (comes with the laptop computer). With the presence of a laptop mouse touchpad, an external mouse is not needed to use a laptop, except in a case where it is malfunctioning or the operator prefers to use external one for some reasons.

The laptop mouse touchpad is usually positioned at the end of the keyboard section of a laptop computer. It is rectangular in shape with two buttons positioned below it. The two buttons/keys are used for left and right clicking just like the external mouse. Some laptops come with four mouse keys. Two placed above the mouse for left and right clicking and two other keys placed below it for the same function.

4. Definition Of Keyboard Shortcuts.

Keyboard shortcuts are defined as a series of keys, most times with combination that execute tasks which typically involve the use of mouse or other input devices.

5. Why You Should Use Shortcuts.

1. One may not be able to use a computer mouse easily because of disability or pain.

2. One may not be able to see the mouse pointer as a result of vision impairment, in such case what will the person do? The answer is SHORTCUT.

3. Research has made it known that Extensive mouse usage is related to Repetitive Syndrome Injury (RSI) greatly than the use of keyboard.

4. Keyboard shortcuts speed up computer users, making learning them a worthwhile effort.

5. When performing a job that requires precision, it is wise that you use the keyboard instead of mouse, for instance, if you are dealing with Text Editing, it is better you handle it using keyboard shortcuts than spending more time doing it with your computer mouse alone.

6. Studies calculate that using keyboard shortcuts allows working 10 times faster than working with the mouse. The time you spend looking for the mouse and then getting the cursor to the position you want is lost! Reducing your work duration by 10 times gives you greater results.

5.1 Ways To Become A Lover Of Shortcuts.

1. Always have the urge to learn new shortcut keys associated with the programs you use.
2. Be happy whenever you learn a new shortcut.
3. Try as much as you can to apply the new shortcuts you learnt.

4. Always bear it in mind that learning new shortcuts is worth it.
5. Always remember that the use of keyboard shortcuts keeps people healthy while performing computer activities.

5.2 How To Learn New Shortcut Keys
1. Do a research on them: quick references (a cheat sheet comprehensively compiled like ours) can go a long way to help you improve.
2. Buy applications that show you keyboard shortcuts every time you execute an action with mouse.
3. Disconnect your mouse if you must learn this fast.
4. Read user manuals and help topics (Whether offline or online).

5.3 Your Reward For Knowing Shortcut Keys.
1. You will get faster unimaginably.
2. Your level of efficiency will increase.
3. You will find it easy to use.
4. Opportunities are high that you will become an expert in what you do.
5. You won't have to go for **Office button**, click **New,** click **Blank and Recent**, and click **Create** just to insert a fresh/blank page. **Ctrl +N** takes care of that in a second.

A Funny Note: Keyboarding and Mousing are in a marital union with Keyboarding being the head, so it will be unfair for anybody to put asunder between them.

5.4 Why We Emphasize On The Use of Shortcuts.

You may never leave your mouse completely unless you are ready to make your brain a box of keyboard shortcuts which will really be frustrating, just imagine yourself learning all shortcuts that go with the programs you use and their various versions. You shouldn't learn keyboard shortcuts that way.

Why we are emphasizing on the use of shortcuts is because mouse usage is becoming unusually common and unhealthy, too. So we just want to make sure both are combined so you can get fast, productive and healthy in your computer activities. All you need to know is just the most important ones associated with the programs you use.

CHAPTER 2.

15 (Fifteen) Special Keyboard Shortcuts.

The fifteen special keyboard shortcuts are fifteen (15) shortcuts every computer user should know.

The following is a list of keyboard shortcuts every computer user should know:

1. **Ctrl + A:** Control A, highlights or selects everything you have in the environment where you are working.

   > *If you are like* **"Wow, the content of this document is large and there is no time to select all of it, besides, it's going to mount pressure on my computer?"** *Using the mouse for this is an outdated method of handling a task like selecting all, Ctrl+A will take care of that in a second.*

2. **Ctrl + C:** Control C copies any highlighted or selected element within the work environment.
    Saves the time and stress which would have been used to right click and click again just to copy. Use ctrl+c.

3. **Ctrl + N:** Control N opens a new window or file.
    Instead of clicking **File**, **New**, **blank/ template** *and another* **click**, *just press* ***Ctrl + N*** *and a fresh page or window will appear instantly.*

4. **Ctrl + O:** Control O opens a new program.
    Use ctrl +O when you want to locate / open a file or program.

5. **Ctrl + P:** Control P prints the active document.
    Always use this to locate the printer dialog box, and thereafter print.

6. **Ctrl + S:** Control S saves a new document or file and changes made by the user.
    Please stop! Don't use the mouse. Just press Ctrl+S and everything will be saved.

7. **Ctrl +V:** Control V pastes copied elements into the active area of the program in use.

Using ctrl+V in a case like this Saves the time and stress of right clicking and clicking again just to paste.

8. **Ctrl + W:** Control W is used to close the page you are working on when you want to leave the work environment.

> ***"There is a way Debby does this without using the mouse. Oh my God, why didn't I learn it then?"*** Don't worry, I have the answer. Debby presses Ctrl+W to close active windows.

9. **Ctrl + X:** Control X cuts elements (making the elements to disappear from their original place). The difference between cutting and deleting elements is that in Cutting, what was cut doesn't get lost permanently but prepares itself so that it can be pasted on another location defined by the user.

> *Use ctrl+x when you think* ***"this shouldn't be here and I can't stand the stress of retyping or redesigning it on the rightful place it belongs".***

10. **Ctrl + Y:** Control Y undoes already done actions.

Ctrl+Z brought back what you didn't need? Press Ctrl+ Y to remove it again.

11. **Ctrl + Z:** Control Z redoes actions.
Can't find what you typed now or a picture you inserted, it suddenly disappeared or you mistakenly removed it? Press Ctrl+Z to bring it back.

12. **Alt + F4:** Alternative F4 closes active windows or items.

*You don't need to move the mouse in order to close an active window, just press **Alt + F4**. Also use it when you are done or you don't want somebody who is coming to see what you are doing.*

13. **Ctrl + F6:** Control F6 Navigates between open windows, making it possible for a user to see what is happening in windows that are active.
Are you working in Microsoft Word and want to find out if the other active window where your browser is loading a page is still progressing? Use Ctrl + F6.

14. **F1:** This displays the help window.

*Is your computer malfunctioning? Use **F1** to find help when you don't know what next to do.*

15. **F12:** This enables user to make changes to an already saved document.

    F12 is the shortcut to use when you want to change the format in which you saved your existing document, password it, change its name, change the file location or destination, or make other changes to it. It will save you time.

Note: The Control (Ctrl) key on Windows and Linux operating system is the same thing as Command (Cmmd) key on a Macintosh computer. So if you replace Control with Command key on a Mac computer for the special shortcuts listed above, you will get the same result.

CHAPTER 3.

Tips, Tricks, Techniques, and Keyboard Shortcuts for use in CorelDraw.

About the program: This is a vector graphics editor developed by Corel Corporation in Jan 16th 1989.

A fresh topic ⌐

Vectorization: Convert to Vector Images with PowerTRACE.

By Steve Bain.

This tutorial has been written for CorelDRAW Graphics Suite X7. While some features might be available in previous releases, the tutorial will be fully applicable to CorelDRAW Graphics Suite X7 and higher.

In this tutorial we'll tackle a bitmap-tracing project that will enable you to quickly produce an accurate two-color vector version of a logo design without the need of a vector converter. Along the way, you'll learn how to use many of the powerful features engineered into PowerTRACE that make the process fast and efficient.

A Primer on Vectorization with PowerTRACE.

If this is your first tracing experience, some advance orientation may help demystify the tools involved. With a bitmap selected in CorelDRAW, PowerTRACE becomes available through the **Trace Bitmap c**ommand on the property bar.

You can instantly trace a selected bitmap and use the default settings by choosing **Quick Trace** from the **Trace Bitmap** list box, which applies the trace without opening the **PowerTRACE** dialog box. Alternatively, you can adjust the settings in the **PowerTRACE** dialog box (shown below). There are six modes that you can choose from, depending on your tracing requirements. The dialog box is divided into two areas. The left side displays a preview of your trace results, while the right side features two option areas.

Across the top of the dialog box are viewing and zooming tools, and across the bottom are the **Undo**, **Redo**, and **Reset** buttons.

If you have previous experience applying bitmap filter effects in CorelDRAW or Corel PHOTO-PAINT®, the PowerTRACE tools will seem like familiar territory. The **Settings** tab is divided into several key areas, including trace controls and trace options. The **Trace result details** area (shown below) provides critical information as you adjust the tracing options. The **Colors** tab includes controls that let you manipulate the color space of the traced results. Follow the tutorial steps below to explore how easily these settings can be applied and modified to produce exactly the tracing results you need.

Before You Begin Converting Your Image.

The bitmap images that you are vectorizing will very likely come from one of two sources: a file that is prepared in a drawing or bitmap-editing application and exported to one of the many available bitmap formats, or a file acquired via an image-capturing device such as a scanner or digital camera.

The source of your bitmap image can significantly influence its inherent quality. Software-generated bitmaps are the best to work with, while scanned images often require some refinement before they can be accurately traced. In the steps that follow, we'll look at both scenarios.

We'll be tracing two bitmaps. Both are CMYK images that have a resolution of 200 dpi and depict the same logo. The first version was exported from a drawing program (CorelDRAW), while the second version was scanned by using a consumer-brand flatbed scanner. Our goal is to produce a usable vector version of the logo prepared in two PANTONE® spot ink colors.

Tracing an Exported Bitmap to Vector.

1. In a new CorelDRAW document, import the first bitmap (shown below). By default, the imported bitmap is selected with the **Pick** tool.

2. Click the **Trace Bitmap** button on the property bar, and choose **Outline Trace > Logo**. The **PowerTRACE** dialog box opens and produces a preliminary trace of the bitmap.

3. The **Smoothing** and **Detail** sliders at the top of the Settings tab are automatically set. The preview window displays a split-screen preview of the Before and After results (as shown below), and the **Trace result details** area indicates that there are 14 curves comprised of 238 nodes and 3 colors.

4. Since the background of our logo is white, PowerTRACE automatically detects and eliminates the surrounding background color. To remove the white area in the interior of the bitmap, enable the

Remove color from entire image check box (shown below). Notice that the **Trace result details** area now indicates that only 8 curves are detected.

5. To check the tracing accuracy, choose **Wireframe Overlay** from the **Preview** list box. Use single left-clicks to zoom in and single right-clicks to zoom out to examine the accuracy of the traced paths. If needed, use the **Transparency** slider to adjust the visibility of the original bitmap. A close look at the upper-left corner (shown below) reveals that the bitmap edges have been accurately traced.

6. Click the Colors tab to examine the color results of the trace, and choose **CMYK** from the **Color Mode** list box. Notice that three CMYK colors are listed at the top (as shown next). Our next step will be to specify these colors as PANTONE spot ink colors.

7. Click the turquoise color in the list, and then click **Edit** to open the **Select Color** dialog box. Click the Palettes tab, and choose PANTONE solid coated from the **Palette** list box. Notice that the PANTONE ink color equivalent of the CMYK value is automatically selected — in this case, PANTONE 7710 C.

8. Click **OK** to close the dialog box and apply PANTONE 7710 C as the new color. Notice that the

color list (shown below) and the trace preview are updated to indicate the ink color you applied.

9. Click the dark blue color in the list, and repeat the previous steps to change the CMYK values of this color to a PANTONE color. You are now ready to accept the trace results.

10 .Click **OK** in the PowerTRACE dialog box to return to your CorelDRAW page. By default, PowerTRACE places the traced objects as a group directly on top of your original bitmap. Drag the group to one side to see both the original bitmap and the traced objects (as shown below). The vector version of your two-color logo is now complete. If you wish, delete the bitmap version from the CorelDRAW page.

Tracing a Scanned Bitmap to Vector.

In the previous steps, we traced a bitmap that originated from a drawing or bitmap-editing application. Next, we'll examine how to vectorize the same logo scanned from a hard copy and saved in the same bitmap format.

1. To begin the vectorization process, import the logo into a new CorelDRAW document, and choose **Detailed logo** from the **Trace Bitmap** flyout on

the property bar. The **PowerTRACE** dialog box opens, and a preliminary trace is immediately produced. Now the **Trace result details** area shows that 113 curves, 7707 nodes, and 15 colors are detected (as shown below). At this point you could move the **Smoothing** and **Detail** sliders to adjust the trace results and likely produce an excellent trace, but here's a chance for you to learn an alternate strategy. Close the PowerTRACE dialog box and return to the bitmap on your page.

2. To refine the scanned image and improve the trace results, we're going to apply a bitmap filter. As you can see, this version of the logo includes scanning imperfections from the hard copy (see below). Eliminating these anomalies will drastically improve the tracing results.

3. Choose **Bitmaps > Blur > Smart Blur** to open the **Smart Blur** dialog box (shown below). Set the slider to 60, and click **OK** to apply the effect. This operation will eliminate most — but not all — of the image's imperfections.

4. Choose **Bitmaps > Noise > Remove Noise** to open the **Remove Noise** dialog box (shown below). Leave the **Auto** check box enabled, and click **OK** to apply the filter. This will eliminate virtually all of the remaining imperfections.

5. With the image selected, choose **Detailed Logo** from the **Trace Bitmap** flyout on the property bar.

6. PowerTRACE opens and displays the trace results. Once again, the **Smoothing** and **Detail** sliders settings are optimized. With **Detailed Logo** selected, the **Trace result details** area now displays 11 curves, 236 nodes, and 9 colors detected (as shown below).

7. Click the **Colors** tab to view the colors detected in the traced image. Hold down **Ctrl**, and click on each of the turquoise colors in the list to select all three colors (as shown below). Click **Merge** to combine these colors into a single color. With the single color still selected, click **Edit** to open the **Select Color** dialog box, and change this color to PANTONE 318 C as you did in the previous steps.

8. Repeat the previous step for the navy blue colors in the list, changing them to a single color. Change the leftover color to PANTONE 274 C, and merge the remaining white colors in the list.

9. Return to the **Settings** tab, and enable the **Remove color from entire image** check box to eliminate the interior background shapes. Notice that the curve count is reduced. You are now ready to accept the trace results.

10. Click **OK** to close the **PowerTRACE** dialog box and return to the CorelDRAW document. Drag the grouped traced objects to the right of the original bitmap and examine the results (shown below). Your tracing task is complete. If you wish, delete the bitmap version from your CorelDRAW page.

Although each bitmap may require its own special treatment, you can see how powerful and easy to use the PowerTRACE features are. In only a few short steps, you've learned how to use PowerTRACE to produce an accurately traced version of a complex logo using only a low-resolution bitmap as the source. Keep in mind that jpg to vector and other raster to vector conversions are equally straightforward.

End of Topic.

A fresh topic

Customize CorelDRAW Graphics Suite to Fit Your Workflow.

By Steve Bain.

This tutorial teaches you how to customize your workspace in CorelDRAW to make it easier to use however you like. When it comes to the creative freedom to radically change your software's user interface, few applications come close to CorelDRAW Graphics Suite. By changing your CorelDRAW or Corel PHOTO-PAINT workspace, you can go wild with custom toolbars, command menus, and shortcuts to create a look and feel to suit your workflow or your tastes.

Besides the cool factor, there's an invaluable practical side to customizing your workspace. It's surprising how quickly each extra moment you spend adjusting tool settings or sifting through options can add up over the course of a task or project. Organizing and optimizing your workspace can yield an invaluable resource that many of us often lack — time.

When it comes to the creative freedom to radically change your software's user interface, few applications come close to CorelDRAW Graphics Suite. By changing your CorelDRAW or Corel PHOTO-PAINT workspace, you can go wild with custom toolbars, command menus, and shortcuts to create a look and feel to suit your workflow or your tastes.

Besides the cool factor, there's an invaluable practical side to customizing your workspace. It's surprising how quickly each extra moment you spend adjusting tool settings or sifting through options can add up over the course of a task or project. Organizing and optimizing your workspace can yield an invaluable resource that many of us often lack — time.

What Makes a Workspace a Workspace?

So, what exactly constitutes a workspace? Essentially, a workspace is a collection of interface settings. It includes the current state and positioning of all dockers, command menus, and toolbars as well as shortcut keys and status bar display. Workspaces also include any customized items you have created such as new menus or custom toolbars.

The workspace files in CorelDRAW Graphics Suite use the XML file format, which means that the files can be easily created, saved, and shared. You can save or share different workspaces for specific designs, layouts, or graphic operations, or create a workspace that emulates other applications. Virtually any interface element can be moved, copied, or deleted, enabling you to personalize your program to suit your own work habits or needs. In this tutorial, we'll explore how to switch between workspaces, customize toolbars and shortcut keys, save your workspace, export your workspace, set document defaults, and restore your application to its original factory settings. That's plenty of ground to cover, so we'd better get started.

Switching Between Workspaces.

CorelDRAW comes with several preset workspaces, each of them optimized for a specific type of workflow (for example, illustration or page layout). To switch from one workspace to another, click **Window > Workspace**, and choose the workspace you want.

Customizing Toolbars Interactively.

Instead of choosing a preset workspace, you can create your own custom workspace by customizing any menu or toolbar. You can use the customization features in the **Options** dialog box, but the interactive method is much more intuitive. All it takes is dragging an item from one menu or toolbar to another.

- To create a new toolbar, hold down **Ctrl + Alt** while dragging an item from a toolbar or menu.
- To copy a button or command, hold down **Ctrl + Alt** while dragging the item to a different toolbar or menu.

- To move a button or command, hold down **Alt** while dragging the item to a new toolbar or menu.
- To delete a button or command, hold down **Alt** while dragging the item off the toolbar or menu.

It's important to press and hold the keys before you begin the mouse action.

When you create a new toolbar, it is automatically named New Toolbar 1 by default. To change the toolbar's name, open the **Options** dialog box (**Ctrl + J**), click **Workspace > Customization > Command Bars** to view the **Command Bars** list, locate your new toolbar, click the toolbar name twice, and type a new name. You can also display or hide toolbars by enabling or disabling the corresponding check boxes.
Toolbars can include elements from various command bars, so you can mix and match elements from any existing toolbar or menu.

You can also add flyouts to your custom toolbars. A flyout is essentially a grouped collection of buttons. Creating new flyouts and copying or moving items from other flyouts requires a little more wrist action.

1. Right-click your custom toolbar, and choose **Customize > [name of toolbar] > Add New Flyout**. A new empty flyout button is added to the toolbar.

2. Open the flyout from which you want to copy a button.
3. Hold down **Ctrl + Alt** while dragging the button from the source flyout until your mouse pointer is over the target flyout. Before releasing the mouse button, you'll see the target flyout open. After it opens, move your pointer onto it, and then release the mouse button.

Customizing Shortcut Keys.

You can access shortcut customization options in the **Options** dialog box by clicking **Workspace > Customization > Commands** and clicking the **Shortcut Keys** tab.

Saving Your Workspace.

After you've customized your menus and toolbars, you can save your custom workspace.

1. Click **Tools > Options (Ctrl + J)**, and click **Workspace** to view the workspace options.

2. Click **New**. In the **New Workspace** dialog box, type a name for your workspace and an optional description. Click **OK** to save the workspace and return to the **Options** dialog box

Your custom workspace is saved and can be accessed from the list. The check mark indicates that it is currently loaded. Click **OK** to close the dialog box.

Exporting Your Workspace.

There are two ways to preserve your custom CorelDRAW or Corel PHOTO-PAINT workspace — either by saving your workspace, or by exporting it. The export operation creates a file that you can email, share with colleagues, or copy to other systems.

1. Right-click any toolbar and choose Customize > Workspace > Export from the popup menu.
2. In the Export Workspace dialog box, choose the workspace settings that you would like to include, and click Save.

3. In the Save As dialog box, enter a name and location for the file, and click Save.
4. In the Export Workspace dialog box, click Close.

Setting Document Defaults.

If you're new to the workspace concept, it may help to know what is and isn't stored in a workspace file. For example, your CorelDRAW workspace does not determine document-level settings. Document settings include defaults such as fill and outline properties for graphic and text objects, a variety of general display preferences, as well as page, ruler, grid, guideline, and style options. These settings provide an extra layer of customization if you need it. You can choose which settings applied to your document to save as defaults for other documents in the **Options** dialog box by choosing the **Document** options. Enable the check marks next to the settings you wish to save.

After you have selected which document settings to save, you can immediately save all current document settings as defaults for new documents by choosing **Tools > Save Settings as Default**. Any currently applied document settings will be saved in your default CorelDRAW.cdt template file and automatically applied to each new document file you create.

Restoring Your Workspace to Factory Defaults.

At this point, you may be wondering how you're going to undo what you've done so far. You can return to the **Options** dialog box anytime and choose a different workspace.

You can also return your workspace to its original factory default state.

1. Close CorelDRAW (or Corel PHOTO-PAINT).
2. Hold the **F8** key, and restart the application. Click **Yes** in the dialog box that appears.

End of Topic.

A fresh topic

Improving the Color of Dull Photos.

By Steve Bain.

In this example, I will take an average photo of a sunflower and transform it into a stunning image in three easy steps.

Step 1: Adjusting the brightness of the image

Open the photo in PaintShop Pro and make sure that the **Edit** workspace is active.

From the **Adjust** menu, select **Smart Photo Fix.**

Since there's a bit of glare on this image, we will reduce the **Overall** brightness to -15.

Next, we'll set the **Shadows** to -20 and the **Highlights** to +20, this will create a nice contrast.

Lastly, we will set the **Focus** to 60 to sharpen the photo a little.

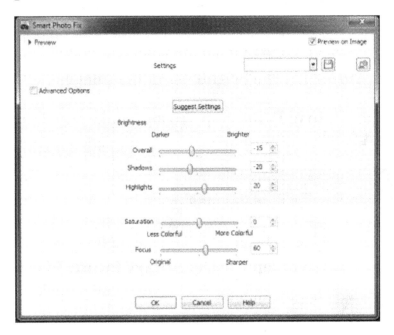

Step 2: Make the color really stand out.

From the **Adjust** menu, select **Hue and Saturation** and then choose **Vibrancy**.

In this example, we'll set the value to **75** to give the photo a rich color.

With the **Preview on Image** check mark selected, you can view the enhancements on the photo while you're working.

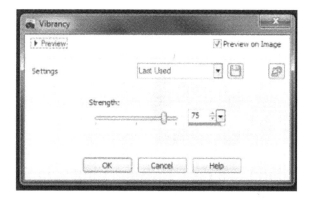

Step 3: Sharpen the image further.

Double click on the **Instant Effect** called **More**

Definition. If the change is not very noticeable, simply repeat the effect by double clicking again.

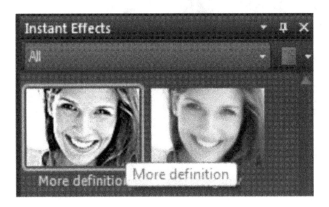

Remember, if there are any marks or imperfections in your image you can always remove those quickly and easily using the **Blemish Fixer** tool.

It's just that easy to make a dull, average photograph into a stunning professional-looking image using Corel PaintShop Pro.

End of Topic.

A fresh topic ⌐⌐→

Keyboard Shortcuts for use in CorelDraw.

The following list is made up of keyboard shortcuts you can use to boost your productivity in CorelDraw.

Task	Shortcut	Description
Align Bottom	B	Aligns selected objects to the bottom

Align Centers Horizontally	E	Horizontally aligns the centers of the selected objects
Align Centers Vertically	C	Vertically aligns the centers of the selected objects
Align Left	L	Aligns selected objects to the left
Align Right	R	Aligns selected objects to the right
Align To Baseline	Alt+F12	Aligns text to the baseline
Align Top	T	Aligns selected objects to the top
Artistic Media	I	Draws curves and applies Preset, Brush, Spray, Calligraphic or Pressure Sensitive effe
Back One	Ctrl+PgDn	Back One
Break Apart	Ctrl+K	Breaks apart the selected object
Brightness/Contrast/Intensity	Ctrl+B	Brightness/Contrast/Intensity...
Bring up Property Bar	Ctrl+Enter	Brings up the Property Bar and gives focus to the first visible item

		that can be tabbed to
Center to Page	P	Aligns the centers of the selected objects to page
Character Formatting	Ctrl+T	Character Formatting
Color Balance...	Ctrl+Shift +B	Color Balance
Combine	Ctrl+L	Combines the selected objects
Contour	Ctrl+F9	Opens the Contour Docker Window
Convert	Ctrl+F8	Converts artistic text to paragraph text or vice versa
Convert Outline To Object	Ctrl+Shift +Q	Converts an outline to an object
Convert To Curves	Ctrl+Q	Converts the selected object to a curve
Copy	Ctrl+C	Copies the selection and places it on the Clipboard
Copy	Ctrl+Inse rt	Copies the selection and places it on the Clipboard

Cut	Ctrl+X	Cuts the selection and places it on the Clipboard
Cut	Shift+Delete	Cuts the selection and places it on the Clipboard
Delete	Delete	Deletes the selected object(s)
Distribute Bottom	Shift+B	Distributes selected objects to the bottom
Distribute Centers Horizontally	Shift+E	Horizontally Distributes the centers of the selected objects
Distribute Centers Vertically	Shift+C	Vertically Distributes the centers of the selected objects
Distribute Left	Shift+L	Distributes selected objects to the left
Distribute Right	Shift+R	Distributes selected objects to the right
Distribute Spacing Horizontally	Shift+P	Horizontally Distributes the space between the selected

Distribute Spacing Vertically	Shift+A	Vertically Distributes the space between the selected objects
Distribute Top	Shift+T	Distributes selected objects to the top
Duplicate	Ctrl+D	Duplicates the selected object(s) and offsets by a specified amount
Duplicate In Place	+	Duplicates the selected object(s) at their current location
Dynamic Guides	Alt+Shift +D	Shows or hides the Dynamic Guides (toggle)
Edit Text...	Ctrl+Shift +T	Opens the Edit Text dialog box
Ellipse	F7	Draws ellipses and circles; double-clicking the tool opens the Toolbox tab of the Option
Envelope	Ctrl+F7	Opens the Envelope Docker Window
Eraser	X	Erases part of a graphic or splits an

		object into two closed paths
Exit	Alt+F4	Exits CorelDRAW and prompts to save the active drawing
Export...	Ctrl+E	Exports text or objects to another format
Font Size Decrease	Ctrl+NU MPAD2	Decreases font size to previous point size
Font Size Increase	Ctrl+NU MPAD8	Increases font size to next point size
Font Size Next Combo Size	Ctrl+NU MPAD6	Increase font size to next setting in Font Size List
Font Size Previous Combo Size	Ctrl+NU MPAD4	Decrease font size to previous setting available in the Font Size List
Forward One	Ctrl+PgU p	Forward One
Fountain Fill...	F11	Applies fountain fills to objects
Freehand	F5	Draws lines and curves in Freehand mode

Full-Screen Preview	F9	Displays a full-screen preview of the drawing
Graph Paper	D	Draws a group of rectangles; double-clicking opens the Toolbox tab of the Options dial
Graphic and Text Styles	Ctrl+F5	Opens the Graphic and Text Styles Docker Window
Group	Ctrl+G	Groups the selected objects
Hand	H	Hand Tool
Horizontal Text C	Ctrl+,	Changes the text to horizontal direction
Hue/Saturation/ Lightness...	Ctrl+Shift +U	Hue/Saturation/Lightness
Import...	Ctrl+I	Imports text or objects
Insert Symbol Character	Ctrl+F11	Opens the Insert Character Docker Window
Interactive Fill	G	Adds a fill to object(s); clicking and dragging on object(s) applies a fountain fill

Lens	Alt+F3	Opens the Lens Docker Window
Linear	Alt+F2	Contains functions for assigning attributes to linear dimension lines
Macro Editor...	Alt+F11	Macro Editor...
Mesh Fill	M	Converts an object to a Mesh Fill object
Micro Nudge Down	Ctrl+DnArrow	Nudges the object downward by the Micro Nudge factor
Micro Nudge Left	Ctrl+Left Arrow	Nudges the object to the left by the Micro Nudge factor
Micro Nudge Right	Ctrl+RightArrow	Nudges the object to the right by the Micro Nudge factor
Micro Nudge Up	Ctrl+UpArrow	Nudges the object upward by the Micro Nudge factor
Navigator	N	Brings up the Navigator window allowing you to navigate to any

		object in the document
New	Ctrl+N	Creates a new drawing
Next Page	PgDn	Goes to the next page
Nudge Down	DnArrow	Nudges the object downward
Nudge Left	LeftArrow	Nudges the object to the left
Nudge Right	RightArrow	Nudges the object to the right
Nudge Up	UpArrow	Nudges the object upw
Open...	Ctrl+O	Opens an existing drawing
Options...	Ctrl+J	Opens the dialog for setting CorelDRAW options
Outline Color...	Shift+F12	Opens the Outline Color dialog box
Outline Pen...	F12	Opens the Outline Pen dialog box
Pan Down	Alt+DnArrow	Pan Down
Pan Left	Alt+LeftArrow	Pan Left
Pan Right	Alt+RightArrow	Pan Right

Pan Up	Alt+UpArrow	Pan Up
Paste	Ctrl+V	Pastes the Clipboard contents into the drawing
Paste	Shift+Insert	Pastes the Clipboard contents into the drawing
Place Inside Container...	Ctrl+1	Places selected object(s) into a PowerClip container object
Polygon	Y	Draws polygons
Position	Alt+F7	Opens the Position Docker Window
Previous Page	PgUp	Goes to the previous page
Print...	Ctrl+P	Prints the active drawing
Properties	Alt+Enter	Allows the properties of an object to be viewed and edited
Record Temporary Macro	Ctrl+Shift+R	Record Temporary Macro
Rectangle	F6	Draws rectangles; double-clicking the tool creates a page frame

Redo	Ctrl+Shift +Z	Reverses the last Undo operation
Refresh Window	Ctrl+W	Redraws the drawing window
Repeat	Ctrl+R	Repeats the last operation
Rotate	Alt+F8	Opens the Rotate Docker Window
Run Temporary Macro	Ctrl+Shift +P	Run Temporary Macro
Save As... S	Ctrl+Shift +	Saves the active drawing with a new name
Save...	Ctrl+S	Saves the active drawing
Scale	Alt+F9 Window	Opens the Scale Docker
Select all	Ctrl+A	Select all object of the active page
Shape	F10	Edits the nodes of an object; double-clicking the tool selects all nodes on the selected
Size	Alt+F10 Window	Opens the Size Docker
Smart Drawing	Shift+S Dbl-click	opens Smart Drawing Tool options; Shift+drag

		backwards over line erases
Snap to Grid	Ctrl+Y	Snaps objects to the grid (toggle)
Snap to Objects	Alt+Z	Snaps objects to other objects (toggle)
Spell Check...	Ctrl+F12	Opens the Spell Checker; checks the spelling of the selected text
Spiral	A	Draws spirals; double-clicking opens the Toolbox tab of the Options dialog
Step and Repeat...	Ctrl+Shift +D	Shows Step and Repeat docker
Stop Recording	Ctrl+Shift +O	Stop Recording
Super Nudge Down	Shift+Dn Arrow	Nudges the object downward by the Super Nudge factor
Super Nudge Left	Shift+Left Arrow	Nudges the object to the left by the Super Nudge factor
Super Nudge Right	Shift+Rig htArrow	Nudges the object to the right by the

		Super Nudge factor
Super Nudge Up	Shift+Up Arrow	Nudges the object upward by the Super Nudge factor
Symbol Manager	Ctrl+F3	Symbol Manager Docker
Text	F8	Adds text; click on the page to add Artistic Text; click and drag to add Paragraph Text
To Back Of Layer	Shift+Pg Dn	To Back Of Layer
To Back Of Page	Ctrl+End	To Back Of Page
To Front Of Layer	Shift+Pg Up	To Front Of Layer
To Front Of Page	Ctrl+Home	To Front Of Page
Toggle Pick State	Ctrl+Space	Toggles between the current tool and the Pick tool
Toggle View	Shift+F9	Toggles between the last two used view qualities
Undo	Ctrl+Z	Reverses the last operation
Undo	Alt+Backspace	Reverses the last operation

Ungroup	Ctrl+U	Ungroups the selected objects or group of objects
Uniform Fill...	Shift+F11	Applies uniform color fills to objects
Use bullets	Ctrl+M	Show/Hide Bullet
Vertical Text	Ctrl+.	Changes the text to vertical
View Manager	Ctrl+F2	Opens the View Manager Docker Window
What's This?	Shift+F1	What's This? Help
Zoom	Z	Zoom Tool
Zoom One-Shot	F2	
Zoom Out	F3	Zoom Out
Zoom To Fit	F4	Zoom To All Objects
Zoom To Page	Shift+F4	Zoom To Page
Zoom To Selection	Shift+F2	Zoom To Selected

Customer's Page.

This page is for customers who enjoyed CorelDraw Keyboard Shortcuts.

Dear beautiful customer, we will feel honoured to have you review this book if you enjoyed or found it useful. We also advise you to get the ebook copy of this book so as to access the numerous links in it. Thank you.

Download Our EBooks Today For Free.

In order to appreciate our customers, we have made some of our titles available at 0.00. They are totally free. Feel free to get a copy of the free titles.

Here are books we give to our customers free of charge:

(A) For Keyboard Shortcuts in Windows check:

Windows 7 Keyboard Shortcuts.

(B) For Keyboard Shortcuts in Office 2016 for Windows check:

Word 2016 Keyboard Shortcuts For Windows.

(C) For Keyboard Shortcuts in Office 2016 for Mac check:

OneNote 2016 Keyboard Shortcuts For Macintosh.

Follow this link to download any of the titles listed above for free.

Note: Feel free to download them from our website or your favorite bookstore today. Thank you.

Other Books By This Publisher.

<u>Note:</u> Titles for single programs under Shortcut Matters series are not part of this list.

S/N	Title	Series
Series A: Limits Breaking Quotes.		
1	Discover Your Key Christian Quotes	Limits Breaking Quotes
Series B: Shortcut Matters.		
1	Windows 7 Shortcuts	Shortcut Matters
2	Windows 7 Shortcuts & Tips	Shortcut Matters
3	Windows 8.1 Shortcuts	Shortcut Matters
4	Windows 10 Shortcut Keys	Shortcut Matters
5	Microsoft Office 2007 Keyboard Shortcuts For Windows.	Shortcut Matters
6	Microsoft Office 2010 Shortcuts For Windows.	Shortcut Matters
7	Microsoft Office 2013 Shortcuts For Windows.	Shortcut Matters
8	Microsoft Office 2016 Shortcuts For Windows.	Shortcut Matters
9	Microsoft Office 2016 Keyboard Shortcuts For Macintosh.	Shortcut Matters
10	Top 11 Adobe Programs Keyboard Shortcuts	Shortcut Matters
11	Top 10 Email Service Providers Keyboard Shortcuts	Shortcut Matters
12	Hot Corel Programs Keyboard Shortcuts	Shortcut Matters

13	Top 10 Browsers Keyboard Shortcuts	Shortcut Matters
14	Microsoft Browsers Keyboard Shortcuts.	Shortcut Matters
15	Popular Email Service Providers Keyboard Shortcuts	Shortcut Matters
16	Professional Video Editing with Keyboard Shortcuts.	Shortcut Matters
17	Popular Web Browsers Keyboard Shortcuts.	Shortcut Matters

Series C: Teach Yourself.

1	Teach Yourself Computer Fundamentals	Teach Yourself
2	Teach Yourself Computer Fundamentals Workbook	Teach Yourself

Series D: For Painless Publishing

1	Self-Publish it with CreateSpace.	For Painless Publishing
2	Where is my money? Now solved for Kindle and CreateSpace	For Painless Publishing
3	Describe it on Amazon	For Painless Publishing

www.ingramcontent.com/pod-product-compliance
Lightning Source LLC
Chambersburg PA
CBHW061033050326
40689CB00012B/2798